Early Irish Monasteries

Conleth Manning

Country House, Dublin

Published in 1995 by
Town House and Country House
Trinity House
Charleston Road
Ranelagh, Dublin 6
Ireland

British Library Cataloguing in Publication Data. A catalogue record for this book is available from the British Library.

ISBN: 0-946172-48-X

Illustration acknowledgements
John Scarry, plate 11; Con Manning, plates 5, 12; Cambridge University Collection of Air Photographs: copyright reserved, photo 22. The remainder of the photographs are copyright of the Office of Public Works. Most of these are the work of Con Brogan, with a smaller number, mainly black and whites, by Jim Bambury. The author would like to thank Con Brogan, John Scarry and Tony Roche for their help with the photographs.

Cover: *The west end of the church of Kilcanonagh on Inishmaan, Aran Islands, Co Galway.*

Series editor: Dr Michael Ryan
Text editor: Elaine Campion
Design & artwork: Bill and Tina Murphy
Colour origination: The Kulor Centre
Printed in Ireland by ßetaprint

CONTENTS

When Christianity spread to Ireland around the fifth century AD, the country was divided into a large number of small kingdoms and lacked any centralised authority. Unlike most of Britain, it had never been conquered by the Romans and had no towns. In the absence of urban centres from which bishops could rule dioceses, as on the Continent, monasteries became popular and powerful in Early Medieval Ireland. Thus the early Irish Church developed along different lines from the Church in most of Europe, and the evidence that survives from early Irish monastic sites reflects this individuality.

The monasteries and the saints who founded them were so much a part of the Irish identity that the most typical and unique features of monastic sites, the high crosses and round towers, were adopted as symbols of Ireland in the nineteenth century. Some of the sites still draw pilgrims in a religious tradition that dates back many centuries, but most visitors today are attracted by their historical associations and particularly by the remarkable carvings on their cross-slabs and crosses and the stark beauty of the buildings. Many of the sites, especially those on islands off the west coast, have the added advantage of being located in areas of outstanding natural beauty.

THE DEVELOPMENT OF MONASTERIES IN IRELAND

We know there were Christians in Ireland by the early fifth century for it is recorded that in the year 431 Pope Celestine I ordained Palladius and sent him as a bishop to the Irish who believed in Christ. The traditional apostle of the Irish is St Patrick, whose missionary work was probably confined mainly to the northern part of the country and to the second half of the fifth century. It is not clear how or when monasticism was introduced to Ireland but from an early stage monasteries took on a special importance in the Irish Church, probably because of the rural nature of Irish society.

Most of the monasteries were founded in the sixth and seventh centuries and their founders came to be regarded as saints. There are hundreds of Irish saints, some associated with many churches and holy wells, such as Brigid or Columcille, while others are associated with only one or two places. Very little historical fact is recorded about most of them, and the saints' Lives, usually written centuries later, throw more light on the times in which they were written than on their subjects. The possession of the burial place and corporeal remains of the founding saint bestowed a particular status to a monastery because of the strong belief in the miraculous power of relics, and monasteries that were not fortunate enough to include the burial place of a saint would have tried to acquire some relic of their patron, whether a bone from the saint's body or some associated object such as a crozier or bell.

In the tradition of the Desert Fathers — the pioneers of Christian monasticism in third- and fourth-century Egypt — some saints founded hermitages or small eremitical communities in out-of-the-way places or on small islands. Most, however, chose populated areas on good land or near important routeways. As time passed, many of the better located monasteries became very wealthy and had large dependent lay communities of monastic tenants, servants and craftworkers. The abbot or ruler of the community was known as the *comarba* (successor), the heir of the founding saint, but as early as the eighth century there are indications that the high ideals of the founders were not being adhered to, at least by some of the rulers; the rule of celibacy was being broken, with evidence of sons succeeding their fathers as abbots, and there were instances of pitched battles between monasteries. The large monasteries became important centres of population, learning, trade and craftsmanship, as well as of religion, with many playing an important part in the political and dynastic struggles of the time. By the tenth and eleventh centuries some of the monasteries were large enough to be classed as towns.

THE LAYOUT OF THE MONASTERY

The early monasteries, both in their layout and organisation, were quite different from those of the Later Medieval period in Ireland. The later foundations usually consisted of a conjoined complex of large masonry buildings formally arranged around a quadrangular cloister garth or enclosure, with the church on one side and the domestic buildings of the monks on the other three sides. Early Irish monasteries, on the other hand, were built largely of timber, and even where the churches were eventually built in stone, the domestic buildings of the monastery would usually still have been constructed of wood or other perishable materials and situated away from the churches, which were free-standing. These domestic buildings, whether built of timber or post and wattle, were possibly located around the *platea* or open court of the monastery to the west of the main church (Pl 1). This, the core of the monastery, with its churches, graveyard and monastic buildings, would have been enclosed from the remainder of the settlement where the monastic tenants and others lived, mostly within the outer enclosure of the monastery. Archaeology has to date thrown little light on the location and form of the monastic buildings, apart from the churches, at the larger sites because the areas involved have usually been disturbed by later church building or by centuries of burial. This gives a disproportionate importance to the smaller, better preserved sites in Kerry and the west of Ireland, where remains of both churches and domestic buildings often survive in stone (Pls 2, 3, 4). It is a matter of debate whether the layout of these small sites can be used to reconstruct the layout of the larger monasteries.

THE EARLY PERIOD (UP TO AD 800)

The monastic buildings of the early period were constructed almost exclusively of perishable materials that have long since disappeared, and at many sites known to have flourished during this time, the only remaining evidence consists of structures and monuments of a later period.

Ogham stones are an early feature of some ecclesiastical sites, especially in the south of the country. These are pillars of stone carved with the ogham script, an alphabet comprising a series of strokes and notches arranged along the edges of the stone (Photo 1). About one third of these stones come from known ecclesiastical sites and, while many may not have been carved for or by Christians, the genesis of the Latin-based ogham alphabet lies, probably, in the same Roman influences that first brought the knowledge of Christianity to Ireland. Some ogham stones have contemporary crosses carved on them (Pl 5), while a few bear inscriptions that are clearly Christian in content. The balance of the evidence indicates that they were commemorative monuments rather than grave markers.

7

Photo 1   *An ogham stone at Kilmalkedar, Co Kerry. The ogham strokes can be seen on two edges of this pillar stone, which is also perforated near the top. In the background is Kilmalkedar Church with its Romanesque doorway and a finial still in position at the apex of the gable.*

The earliest cross-inscribed pillars were likewise not erected to mark individual graves (Photo 2). Some display remnants of the chi-rho, the first letters of Christ's name in Greek, incorporated into a cross with or without a

8

Photo 2   *A cross-inscribed pillar at Glencolumbkille, Co Donegal.*

circle. Other early examples, especially in Kerry, have spiral ornament associated with the cross and may be as early as the sixth or seventh centuries. A particularly fine example is the pillar at Reask on the Dingle peninsula in

9

County Kerry (Pl 6), which also has a contracted inscription: DNE, for the Latin *Domine* (O Lord).

At the Reask site, an oratory, cemetery, cross-inscribed pillars and domestic buildings were contained within a subcircular enclosure delimited by a stone wall. Earlier than most of the structures was an occupation layer that contained fragments of wine jars or *amphorae* imported from the East Mediterranean area in the fifth or sixth centuries. At Reask, lintel graves (lined and covered with slabs) and the remains of a stone shrine for relics belong to the earlier phases of the site, while some of the drystone buildings, including the oratory, are of later date, possibly after AD 800 (Photo 3).

The very small area of Church Island in Valencia Harbour, Co Kerry, is fully taken up by a tiny ecclesiastical site enclosed within a wall (Pl 2). Excavations have revealed the drystone oratory to be secondary, as a number of burials predated it and postholes beneath its floor indicate a pre-existing wooden oratory. There was a shrine here also and a pillar with both a cross and an ogham inscription, as well as two domestic structures.

Photo 3 *The oratory and cemetery area at Reask, Co Kerry, during excavation. Note the earlier lintel grave within the remains of the rectangular oratory, and other graves to the left of it.*

10

THE WEST COAST SITES

There is a remarkable series of well-preserved small monasteries, hermitages and church sites along the west coast and on the islands off it. Common features of these sites are cross-inscribed pillars or slabs, small stone churches or oratories, circular stone huts or cells (*clochán* in Irish), often with corbelled drystone roofs, a stone shrine or *leacht* and an enclosing wall.

Perhaps the most remarkable of all is the well-preserved monastery of Skellig Michael, which is perched on a precipitous rocky island some miles off the Kerry coast. Here there are at least six *clocháns*, two oratories and the remains of a church built on man-made terraces clinging to the sloping rockface some one hundred and eighty metres above sea level (Pl 7). The corbelled roofs of the oratories and most of the *clocháns* are still intact, as is the main set of stone steps leading from sea level up to the monastery. Recent research has uncovered the remains of an even more remote hermitage on the steeper and higher south peak of the island.

The drystone corbelled oratories, which are sometimes compared to an upturned boat and of which Gallarus Oratory on the Dingle peninsula is the best preserved and finest example, are almost exclusively a County Kerry phenomenon (Pls 4, 5). Formerly they were seen as the earliest type of stone church in Ireland, predating all mortared examples, but now they are accepted as a localised group belonging mainly to the later part of the Early Medieval period and overlapping chronologically with mortared stone churches. It has been suggested that Gallarus was built as late as the twelfth century, but this is probably an over-reaction to the previous insistence on a very early dating.

The Aran Islands off Galway have a fine collection of early ecclesiastical sites, the most famous being St Enda's monastery at Killeany on Inishmore (Photo 4). According to tradition, St Enda taught many other saints here, who in turn founded their own monasteries throughout the country. Inishmurray, off the Sligo coast, has a remarkable small monastic site enclosed within a massive cashel wall, which has lead to speculation that the monastery was founded within a pre-existing stone fort (Pl 3). As well as a large and varied collection of cross-slabs, there are fine examples here of a monument type known as a *leacht*. This is a small square stone platform or altar, which often has a cross-inscribed pillar erected on it (Photo 5).

11

Photo 4 *The church at Tighlagheany, near Killeany on Inishmore, Aran Islands, Co Galway. The eastern end of this church, with its antae (projecting side walls) and massive facing stones, is ancient. The remainder, including the doorway, may be as late as the seventeenth century.*

Photo 5 *A leacht with a cross-pillar set on it at Inishmurray, Co Sligo. Leachts are square stone platforms which sometimes served as stations on the pilgrims' rounds. Their origin and purpose are not fully understood.*

12

Island sites are not exclusively a western phenomenon and examples are found on coastal and lake islands in other parts. Hermitage sites have also been found in what were remote or uninhabited places, such as mountain peaks or valleys or islands in bogs.

LARGE MONASTERIES

Some of the monasteries founded around the sixth century (Photo 6) gradually grew in size and wealth to become major centres of population in a society where towns were otherwise unknown, apart from the few tenth-century and later Viking towns. The largest foundations became the centres of federations of monasteries and they also controlled other types of churches. As early as AD 700 there were disputes between these large federations over the control of smaller churches and there are records of battles between monasteries. Naturally the monasteries became pawns in the political power struggles of the time, and

Photo 6 *The main group of monuments and focal centre of the monastery at Glendalough, Co Wicklow. The largest building is the cathedral, with the round tower to its north-west. The church known as St Kevin's Kitchen, with its own mini round tower projecting from the stone roof, is on the left.*

13

even before the Vikings first appeared, Irish kings were raiding monasteries in the territories of their rivals. This practice increased with the arrival of the Vikings, but despite frequent raids the monasteries were able to recover quickly and generally continued to flourish.

The larger monasteries are spread throughout the country and are usually situated on good land or close to important routeways. There is, however, a particular concentration of monasteries in the south midlands, an area on the border between provinces and speckled with bogs.

Most of the monuments that can be seen today on these sites are from the later part of the Early Medieval period. As well as a number of churches, the most significant sites also include a round tower and crosses and cross-inscribed graveslabs. The domestic buildings of the monks, the scriptoria, the guesthouses and the houses and other buildings of the dependent community have all vanished because they were built of perishable materials. Traces of the enclosing banks or walls that surrounded the sites can sometimes be detected, which help in assessing the extent of the settlements.

CHURCHES

The earliest Irish churches were of timber or other perishable materials and it is only in the late eighth and ninth centuries that we first find references in the annals to stone churches — and then only at major centres such as Armagh and Kells. The change from timber to stone in the construction of churches may have been instigated by the increase in the numbers of raids, burnings and pilferings of church property after the first wave of Viking raids in the ninth century. Around this time also many stone high crosses were erected, some of which possibly replaced earlier wooden examples. The stone church of Clonmacnoise was built by the High King Flann and Abbot Colmán in 909 and is the oldest surviving dated stone church in the country. Now termed a cathedral, it is still the largest church at Clonmacnoise (Pl 1), and though much altered in later times, most of its surviving north, east and west walls are original. The building of stone churches became more common in the tenth century, and by the eleventh century they had become the norm. Romanesque-style churches in Ireland belong to the twelfth century.

Irish pre-Romanesque mortared stone churches mostly follow a set pattern. They were simple rectangular buildings with sides in proportion, between 1:1.3 and 1:2. Natural lighting was sparse, with only a small window centred in the east gable wall and another towards the east end of the south wall (Photo 7). The single doorway was centred in the west gable wall and was often a flat-headed, lintelled opening, sometimes wider at the base than at the top (Photos 8, 9; Pl 8). One of the most distinctive features of these buildings was a high steeply pitched roof which was carried right over the gables to have its ends supported on projecting portions of the side walls, known as *antae* (Photos 4, 8), or on corbels projecting east and west from the corners (Photo 7; Pl 8). These tall, steep gables, rising from the inner edges of the antae or corbels, rarely survive

Photo 7   *A view from the south-east of Templemacduagh, Inishmore, Aran Islands. The chancel is an addition to a simple rectangular church with antae. Note the corbels (projecting stones) at the corners of the chancel and the original steep gable line. The projecting parapet on the south wall of the chancel is a Later Medieval addition.*

7

8

9

Photo 8   *The west façade of Templemacduagh, Kilmurvey, Inishmore, Aran Islands, showing its plain lintelled doorway and its projecting side walls. This style of masonry, using large facing stones, is sometimes called Cyclopean.*

Photo 9   *The west gable of the church at Kiltiernan, Co Galway, showing the fine limestone masonry and the lintelled doorway. The broken-off remains of antae can be seen on the right side.*

15

because many were truncated to suit the lower pitched roofs of Later Medieval builders.

The churches are very small in comparison with Later Medieval and modern churches and many were enlarged in later times. They range from structures that could be classed as oratories, such as Temple Ciarán at Clonmacnoise, which measures 3.8 by 2.8 m (12½ x 9 ft) internally, to the largest, the cathedral at Clonmacnoise, which originally measured 18.8 by 10.7 m (61½ x 35 ft) internally. Most of the churches would fall somewhere in the middle or lower end of this range; examples such as Clonmacnoise or Glendalough cathedrals are exceptional. It appears that rather than building one much larger church as the population of a monastery grew, smaller churches were added.

Some of the churches display a style of masonry which is often described as Cyclopean, whereby the wall appears to have been built of massive stones. Closer examination reveals that these are relatively thin slabs on edge forming only a facing to the wall, but the effect is very impressive. Some facing stones are, however, truly massive, as at Tighlagheany on the Aran Islands, where one example is over three metres long (Photo 4). This is a sophisticated rather than a primitive style of building which requires a strong mortared core for stability, and it is interesting that our earliest dated stone church, Clonmacnoise cathedral, is not built in this style. Cyclopean masonry may, therefore, be largely a phenomenon of the later tenth and eleventh centuries and confined to areas where suitable stone, especially limestone, was available to enable the builders to create the effect of massivity.

Surviving decoration on these churches is very rare prior to the Romanesque phase and is usually confined to an architrave around the doorway or a cross above it (Photo 10). However, decoration in media other than stone is likely to have adorned these buildings, at least in the interior. It is possible that some had internal mural paintings or moulded stucco-work, though hard evidence of this is lacking. Woodwork and tapestries may also have embellished the interiors. Some certainly had elaborate altars and reliquaries. An idea of the decoration and layout of one of the greater and more important churches is given in Cogitosus's seventh-century Life of St Brigit. The author describes a large, probably wooden, church at Kildare, where the bodies of Conleth and Brigit were enshrined in ornate tombs adorned with precious metals and gems, one to

16

cont. p 29

Pl 1   *The main group of monuments at Clonmacnoise, viewed from the round tower. The
largest building is the cathedral, built originally in 909. To the right is Temple Dowling and
the South Cross, and in the foreground the Cross of the Scriptures.*

17

Pl 2   *An aerial view of Church Island, Valencia, Co Kerry, with its ruined drystone oratory, round beehive cell or* clochán, *and other features, all enclosed by a stone wall. Excavation showed that both buildings were preceded by wooden counterparts.*

Pl 3   *The monastery at Inishmurray, Co Sligo, with its massive enclosing wall, viewed from the air. There has been speculation that the enclosure was an earlier stone fort taken over by the monks.*

18

Pl 4   *The oratory at Gallarus, Co Kerry. This is the most complete and perfect example of a stone-roofed oratory built entirely without mortar. The technique of corbelling the walls inwards until they meet is similar to that used in the circular beehive huts.*

Pl 5   *A ruined stone oratory at Ballymorereagh on the Dingle Peninsula, Co Kerry, with a cross-inscribed ogham stone in front of it. The original finial stone of the roof has been reset on the ruined wall above the door.*

19

Pl 6   A cross-inscribed pillar stone at Reask, Co Kerry. The cross, with widely expanded terminals, is in a rounded frame, beneath which is a composition with spiral ornament. The inscription to the left reads DNE, a contraction for Domine *(O Lord)*.

Pl 7   An aerial view of the main group of monuments on Skellig Michael. Huddled together on a partly artificial terrace are an oratory, the remains of a church, and six stone beehive cells or clocháns, *all but one with their drystone roofs intact.*

(Facing page)
Pl 8   The west end of the small church of Kilcanonagh on Inishmaan, Aran Islands, Co Galway. Note the plain lintelled doorway and the original steeply pitched gable, over which the roof would have been carried with its end rafters resting on corbels, such as the intact one on the right. The side walls were raised in later times.

20

Pl 9 *Cormac's Chapel, Cashel, Co Tipperary, is the best preserved Romanesque church in Ireland. Romanesque architecture appears to have been associated with the twelfth-century reform movement in the Irish Church, which brought about the end of the early monasteries.*

22

Pl 10   *The round tower at Kilmacduagh, Co Galway, with the cathedral to the right. The west end of the cathedral is at latest eleventh century, with its lintelled doorway, roof corbels and steeply pitched gable.*

23

Pl 11   The round tower at Glendalough, Co Wicklow. Its high-level doorway is visible above the bush to the left. There are four windows, facing north, south, east and west, at the top floor, where the bells would have been rung.

Pl 12   The round tower and ruined church at Tullaherin, Co Kilkenny. The church, which is partly early in date, has antae at the east end of the nave, and is situated unusually close to the round tower.

(Facing page)
Pl 13   The south cross at Ahenny, Co Tipperary. Dating probably from the early ninth century, this type of high cross with overall abstract ornament is thought to be derived from metal-encased wooden crosses. The large bosses are placed where functional rivets would have held such a wooden cross together.

24

(Facing page)
Pl 14   *The east face of Muiredach's Cross at Monasterboice, Co Louth. The carvings in panels on the shaft represent scenes from the Bible, such as Adam and Eve, Cain and Abel, David and Goliath, etc. At the centre of the cross Christ stands in judgement on the Last Day, dividing the blessed from the damned.*

Pl 15   *The unfinished cross at Kells, Co Meath, with the round tower in the background. This is informative in showing the way the sculptor planned his work.*

27

Pl 16   *A detail of the tall narrow base of the high cross at Moone, Co Kildare, showing from the top: the three children in the fiery furnace, the flight into Egypt and the loaves and fishes.*

28

cont. from p 16

Photo 10   *The lintelled doorway of Clonamery Church, Co Kilkenny. Note the architrave or raised band around the doorway and the Maltese-type cross above it.*

the left and the other to the right of the altar. There were crowns of gold and silver hanging above them, and the account also mentions carved images, paintings and partition walls made of boards.

Churches with clearly differentiated chancels are more commonly a feature

29

Photo 11 *The interior of Reefert Church, Glendalough, Co Wicklow. The chancel is contemporary with the nave, and an unusual feature of this and Trinity Church, also at Glendalough, is the plain chancel arch spanning the full width of the chancel.*

(Facing page) Photo 12 *The ornately carved twelfth-century Romanesque doorway at Killeshin, Co Laois. There are four orders or steps on the sides and arch, and the gable feature above the arch is common among Irish Romanesque doorways.*

of the twelfth-century Romanesque and later styles in Ireland. There are, however, a number of plain nave-and-chancel churches at Glendalough which probably pre-date the flowering of the Romanesque in Ireland and may belong to the eleventh or very early twelfth centuries (Photo 11).

With the arrival of the Romanesque style, stone carving was extensively used for the first time in Irish church architecture. The stone-roofed and twin-towered Cormac's Chapel at Cashel, Co Tipperary (Pl 9), is the finest surviving example of this style in Ireland, but it is by no means typical of Irish Romanesque churches, which are generally much less elaborate. Often the doorway and chancel arch are the only features that distinguish them from earlier churches. Sometimes these features were simply added to an earlier church. The semi-circular or rounded arch is always used and both the arches and sides are usually in a number of orders or steps, with carvings concentrating on the arch stones and capitals in particular. Some of the doorways have small external triangular gable features over the arch, and fine examples can be seen at Killeshin, Co Laois (Photo 12) and Clonfert, Co Galway. All of these churches were quite small, but much larger churches

with transepts and arcaded aisles were also being introduced around this time by the new continental orders, such as the Cistercians, whose first Irish abbey, Mellifont in Co Louth, was founded in 1142.

ROUND TOWERS AND SHRINES

The tall, slender, free-standing round towers with conical caps which are still such a striking feature of many of the more important monasteries (Pls 10, 11) date from the tenth to the early twelfth centuries. The Irish name for them in the historical sources, *cloigtheach*, means a bell-house and indicates that this was their main function. Most have high-level doorways requiring a ladder for access, and historical references indicate that they were sometimes used for storing valuables and as a refuge during raids. The earliest mention of a round tower in the annals is of an example at Slane, Co Meath, of which no trace survives. This reference states that in the year 950 it was set on fire by the foreigners of Dublin, and burned in it were the founder's crozier, a bell and a large number of people, including the lector (reader) of the monastery.

Round towers are normally situated to the west of the principal church, with the doorway of the tower facing the church. There are usually offsets or ledges on the inside which would have held the wooden floors. Ladders would again have given access from floor to floor, with occasional windows providing light. At the highest level there were four windows, from which hand bells would have been rung. As many of the towers are of great height, over thirty metres in some cases, they were sometimes hit and damaged by lightning. The annals record that the *cloigtheach* at Telach Innmuinn in the ancient territory of Ossory, probably the round tower at Tullaherin, Co Kilkenny (Pl 12), was struck by lightning in 1121, causing a stone to fall from it and kill a student in the church.

The twelfth-century Romanesque-style round towers were the last to be built and some, such as Timahoe in Co Laois, have fine Romanesque doorways (Photo 13).

The cult of relics was very important throughout the Early Medieval period and an important feature of most of these sites must have been the grave or shrine of the founding saint, or at least a reliquary of some sort. Simple slab shrines, similar in shape to a small tent (Photo 14), are prominent features of

Photo 13 *The round tower at Timahoe, Co Laois, has a beautiful Romanesque doorway, which is 4.7m (15¹/₂ ft) above ground level. It is a very elaborate doorway with heads carved on capitals and bases.*

Photo 14 *A view of the slab shrine at St Cronan's Church, Termon, Co Clare. This is a simple structure formed of two rectangular slabs leaning together, with a triangular slab at each end. It would have contained the bones of a saint.*

33

some of the west coast sites, especially in Kerry. Killabuonia, Co Kerry, has a circular hole in one of the triangular end slabs through which devotees could no doubt touch the relics or at least the clay over the saint's grave. Other stone shrines took the form of boxes with grooved stone pillars at the corners into which the side slabs slotted, while some masonry or solid stone house-shaped shrines, such as at Clones, Co Monaghan, are known from the north of the country. Oratory-type structures at important sites such as Clonmacnoise and Ardmore in Co Waterford are traditionally regarded as the founding saint's burial place and probably served much the same purpose as the smaller shrines in being the main focus of devotion and pilgrimage.

CROSSES AND CROSS-SLABS

A free-standing cross or cross-inscribed pillar in wood or stone was probably a feature of many church sites from the earliest days of Christianity in Ireland. Adamnán, in his Life of St Columba written about AD 700, mentions a cross having been set in a millstone at Columba's great monastery of Iona off the west coast of Scotland long before his time. This may have been wooden, for some of our earliest high crosses such as those at Ahenny, Co Tipperary, appear to be copies in stone of metal-encased wooden crosses (Pl 13). It is likely therefore that before the stone high crosses became fashionable in the ninth century, large wooden crosses were common on Irish ecclesiastical sites.

The 'ringed' or Celtic cross is the most common high cross form and it appears to have become particularly popular in the ninth century. The Ahenny group of crosses, from the early ninth century, is richly decorated with abstract ornamentation, including spiral, fret and interlace patterns, and the figured scenes are confined mainly to the base of the cross (Pl 13). The great scriptural crosses from the later ninth and early tenth centuries are major monuments in the history of European art. The scenes depicted on them are mainly from the Old and New Testaments and fine examples of these crosses can be seen at Monasterboice, Co Louth and Kells, Co Meath (Pls 14, 15). The cross at Moone in Co Kildare (Pl 16) is a fine example of a local school of sculpture in the Barrow valley.

The crosses were public monuments rather than grave markers. Some appear to have stood around the central meeting place or *platea* of the monastery (Pl 1) while others marked the boundaries or limits of sanctuary. Some have inscriptions which, as well as helping to date them, show that they were in some cases the result of royal patronage. The damaged inscription on the Cross of the Scriptures at Clonmacnoise refers to the High King Flann and Abbot Colmán, who together built the cathedral in 909.

There is a separate group of twelfth-century high crosses that are often associated with contemporary Romanesque churches. They generally have large-scale figures of Christ and a bishop, reflecting the enhanced status of the bishop under the twelfth-century reform and reorganisation of the Irish Church. Good examples can be seen at Dysart O'Dea and Kilfenora in Co Clare (Photo 15).

Photo 15 *The high cross at Dysart O'Dea, Co Clare (twelfth century). Note the large scale of the figures of Christ and a bishop on this cross in contrast with the figured scenes on earlier crosses.*

35

Stone slabs with inscribed crosses are known from many early ecclesiastical sites. Small plain examples, such as those from Toureen Peakaun, Co Tipperary, which have inscriptions with personal names only, may be as early as the seventh century (Photo 16). However, the bulk of the slabs from other sites are likely to date from the eighth to twelfth centuries (Photos 17, 18, 19, 20). Those with inscriptions almost invariably follow the formula 'O̅R̅ DO X' ('A prayer for X'). With up to seven hundred complete or fragmentary examples, Clonmacnoise has by far the largest collection of these slabs, and while they may not all be grave markers, the majority could certainly be described as such (Photos 18, 19). Despite the large numbers, none of those at Clonmacnoise is still in its original position, but examples at Reefert Church at Glendalough may be in their original locations, lying flat on graves, with other slabs and small crosses serving as upright headstones.

(Facing page)
Photo 17   *An ornate cross-inscribed slab at Tullylease, Co Cork. The Latin inscription asks for a prayer for Berechtuine.*

36

Photo 16   *A small cross-slab from Toureen Peakaun, Co Tipperary. The inscription, partly in Irish and partly in Latin, reads FINÁN PUER (Finán the boy).*

Photo 18 *A cross-slab at Clonmacnoise, Co Offaly, with a ringed Latin cross bearing ornate spiral terminals. The inscription reads OR DO THUATHAL (A prayer for Tuathal).*

(Facing page) Photo 19 *A cross-slab at Clonmacnoise, Co Offaly, with ornate expanded terminals. The inscription reads OR DO MAELMHÍCHÍL (A prayer for Maelmhíchíl).*

Photo 20   *A cross-slab at Gallen, Co Offaly, carved with a ringed cross in high relief. Serpents emanating from a spiral at the centre feed on human heads at the terminals and on a full figure on the shaft.*

(Facing page)
Photo 21   *A plain solid-ringed granite cross at Nurney, Co Carlow. Such plain crosses may have had decoration painted on them, just as the carvings on the more ornate crosses are likely to have been painted originally.*

ENCLOSURES

A feature common to virtually all early ecclesiastical sites was an enclosure, normally round or oval in shape and considerably larger than the modern graveyard that frequently marks these sites. The enclosing element was usually a bank and fosse (ditch), but sometimes it consisted of a stone wall, such as that at Moyne, near Shrule, Co Mayo, which encloses an area averaging 130 m

(426 ft) in diameter (Photo 22). At Seirkieran in Co Offaly, earthen banks and ditches almost completely enclose an area of some ten acres. In some cases only segments of the enclosure survive, either as upstanding features or merely as curving field fences. The use of aerial photography has in some instances revealed traces of the enclosures as low earthworks or cropmarks. Aerial photographs suggest that many of the larger sites had an inner and an outer enclosure. The inner enclosure would seem to have contained the religious core

Photo 22 *An aerial photograph of the early ecclesiastical enclosure at Moyne, near Shrule, Co Mayo. The enclosing element is a large wall up to 3m (10 ft) thick. The modern graveyard, with its ruined church, takes up only a fraction of the enclosure, where other internal divisions can be traced.*

43

of the monastery, while most of the associated settlement was contained within the outer one.

It is to this outer area that the attention of archaeologists has tended to be directed in recent years. Excavation at Armagh and Clonmacnoise has revealed intensive settlement outside the core area, which supports the classification of some of these larger monasteries as towns. At Clonmacnoise, traces of circular houses have been found and evidence that a variety of trades and crafts were practised, including antler-working or comb-making and iron-, bronze-, silver- and gold-working. Evidence for domestic activities such as the drying and grinding of corn has also been found. By the ninth century many of these sites had become major centres of trade and craftsmanship, making them profitable places to plunder and important locations for kings to control, both from an economic and a political point of view.

DECLINE OF THE MONASTERIES

The twelfth century saw great changes in the organisation of the Church in Ireland and the consequent collapse of the old native monastic system. The Church was reorganised into dioceses ruled by bishops, and monastic orders, such as the Augustinians and Cistercians, were introduced from the Continent for the first time. Both processes were accelerated by the Anglo-Norman conquest of most of the country which began in the later twelfth century and continued into the thirteenth. Some of the major monasteries became episcopal sees, others adopted the Augustinian rule, while still others were demoted to serve as parish churches. Some of the monasteries have survived as towns to the present day, such as Armagh, Kildare, Kells (Co Meath), Killaloe (Co Clare) and Derry, while others gradually became deserted, such as Clonmacnoise, Durrow, Kilmacduagh and Monasterboice.

In many parts of Ireland the saints associated with these sites are still revered locally and the holy well (sometimes a short distance from the ecclesiastical site) is often resorted to for devotion and cures, showing how the living tradition survives even when little else remains.

VISITING THE SITES

Most of the more important sites are in the care of the Office of Public Works or, if in Northern Ireland, of the Department of the Environment and are open to the public. For information on opening times and charges, contact the local tourist office or Visitor Services Section, Office of Public Works, 51 St Stephen's Green, Dublin 2. Tel. 01-6613111, or The Archaeological Survey, 5–33 Hill Street, Belfast BT1 2LA. Tel. 0232-23500. Some others in Church of Ireland ownership are still in use and access to them may be limited. In such cases and for information about boat services to islands, local tourist offices should be consulted.

Antae: A feature of early Irish churches whereby the side walls were continued a short distance beyond the gable ends.

Capital: The enlarged and often decorated portion at the top of a column or pier, just below the springing of an arch.

Chancel: The eastern section of a church, containing the altar. The chancel is usually narrower than the nave or main body of the church, from which it is separated by a chancel arch.

Corbel: A stone projecting from a wall face, designed to support a widening of the wall or a wooden beam.

Cropmark: In cultivated fields, archaeological features below ground sometimes cause differential growth in crops which, when viewed from the air, can betray the presence of an otherwise invisible site or feature.

Earthwork: A mound, bank or other man-made feature formed of earth.

Finial stone: The stone at the apex of the gable of a church, which can either be in the form of a cross or of the crossed-over ends of roof rafters.

Fosse: A ditch or trench of a defensive nature, such as that from which the material of a defensive bank would have been dug.

Lintel grave: A grave closely lined with upright slabs and covered with other slabs (lintels) resting on side slabs.

Nave: The main body of a church, usually cut off from the chancel by a chancel arch.

Romanesque: A style of architecture using the Roman or semi-circular arch, which was in vogue in Ireland in the twelfth century.

Stucco-work: Decorative moulded plaster on walls or ceilings.

Transept: The cross-arm element of a church which is cruciform in plan.

46

de Paor, Máire and Liam. *Early Christian Ireland*, Thames and Hudson, London, 1958.

Edwards, Nancy. *The Archaeology of Early Medieval Ireland*, Batsford, London, 1990.

Fanning, Thomas. 'Excavation of an Early Christian cemetery and settlement at Reask, Co Kerry', *Proceedings of the Royal Irish Academy*, vol 81c (1981), 67–172.

Harbison, Peter. 'How old is Gallarus Oratory', *Medieval Archaeology*, vol 14 (1970), 34–59.
   The High Crosses of Ireland, Dr Rudolf Habelt GMBH, Bonn, 1992.
   Guide to National and Historic Monuments of Ireland, Gill and Macmillan, Dublin, 1992.

Hughes, Kathleen, and Hamlin, Ann. *The Modern Traveller to the Early Irish Church*, SPCK, London, 1977.

Leask, Harold G. *Irish Churches and Monastic Buildings, 1. The First Phases and the Romanesque*, Dundalgan Press, Dundalk, 1977.

Lionard, Pádraig. 'Early Irish grave slabs', *Proceedings of the Royal Irish Academy*, vol 61c (1961), 95–169.

Manning, Conleth. *Clonmacnoise*, Office of Public Works, Dublin, 1994.

O'Kelly, Michael J. 'Church Island near Valencia, County Kerry', *Proceedings of the Royal Irish Academy*, vol 59c (1958), 57–136.

Ryan, Michael (ed). *Irish Archaeology Illustrated*, Country House, Dublin, 1994.

Swan, Leo. 'Monastic Proto-towns in Early Medieval Ireland: The evidence of aerial photography, plan analysis and survey' in H B Clarke and A Simms (eds), *The Comparative History of Urban Origins in non-Roman Europe*, 2 vols, British Archaeological Reports, Oxford, 1985.

INDEX